Sometimes I Fly

Tim Goldthorpe

Stairwell Books

Published by Stairwell Books
70 Barbara Drive
Norwalk
CT 06851 USA

Sometimes I Fly©2014 Tim Goldthorpe and Stairwell Books

All rights reserved. No part of this publication may be reproduced, stored in or introduced into a retrieval system, or transmitted, in any form, or by any means (electronic, mechanical, photocopying, recording, e-book or otherwise) without the prior written permission of the author. Any person who does any unauthorised act in relation to this publication may be liable to criminal prosecution and civil claims for damages. Purchase of this book in e-book format entitles you to store the original and one backup for your own personal use; it may not be resold, lent or given away to other people and it may only be purchased from the publisher or an authorised agent.

This book is sold subject to the condition that it shall not, by way of trade or otherwise, be lent, resold, hired out, or otherwise circulated without the author's prior consent in any form of binding or cover other than that in which it is published and without a similar condition including this condition being imposed on the subsequent purchaser.

ISBN: 978-1-939269-15-7

Printed and bound in the in the UK by Russell Press

Edited by Alan Gillott

Introduction

Tim Goldthorpe was born in Uganda on 3rd of June 1953. His idyllic life on the campus of Kampala University ended when his parents decided to return their family to England as Ugandan politics had become dangerous. He has been writing since the age of six. Gradually bipolar schizophrenia developed and he has been a sufferer for forty years. This collection could have been called *To Hell and Back Again* but it hasn't been that awful, really! His conviction is that there is always hope.

Patricia Goldthorpe

Thanks to Mr. Thomas who encouraged me to write

Table of Contents

Arrangement	1
God Against Rock 'n' Roll	2
Retirement	3
Height of Summer	4
I'm not in love	5
Golden Orioles	6
'Hejira' in Horncastle	7
HAIKU	8
Hitching alone	10
Itlopa	11
Lecture in a dream	12
Life story/Lunaire	13
Love in Green	14
Love poem no.14	15
Report	16
Peace	17
Overlord, your fence is too high	18
On a Midsummer Eve	20
Midsummer Marriage	21
Man on the road	22
A Bee on a Lupin	23
Alone	24
A Quick One	25
Autumn	26
Benedict	27
Cities	28
Blackpool	29
Cow Bank	30
Don't Do Drugs	31
Eternity	32
Falling in love on buses and trains	33
26/4/94	34
1967 Revisited	35
Where there's Help there's Hope	37
walking man	38
More from the Smoke Room	39

Wait for no man	40
Voice	41
TIME	42
Two Homes	43
The unknown musician	44
The World Inside Your Eye	45
The Snake	46
The Moose	47
The Oak and the Elm	48
The evening of two angels	49
Sunday at 6	50
Song of the Seasons	51
The Devil Came Up Here	52
Love in the afternoon	53
Winter	54
Schizophrenia	55
Rising dreams like	56
Machine	57
In an Asian Restaurant	58
Afternoon Daymare	59
After Caravaggio	60
Music stroke Light	62
Alchemy	63
In appreciation of your *'lofty pathos'*	64
40 line poem/music in 40 parts	65
Three Ages	67
Meeting with Pan	68
thinking man	69
Community Care	70
When I saw your face again	71
Sunday Afternoons	72
Scene	74
Skyscene	75

Arrangement

You are making
a flower arrangement.
I am making a poem.
Someday I will arrange flowers for you
while you write a love song for me,
but, for now,
you are writing a poem
and I am growing a flower.
We are caught up
in the dizzy heights
of love, wine, laughter and music,
together,
now,
in an ordinary room
in a city street...
The flowers will look nice
on my grandmother's table.
I hope you like the poem.

God Against Rock 'n' Roll

Shadrach, Meshach and Abednego
Were all three listening to the sound below.
The sound was emanating from an old tin can
It was the best rock 'n' roll in this whole damn land.

Moses and Aaron were called upon to fight
Legislation that affected their natural right
To listen to Rock music any hour of day or night
And dance a little, strut a little, without taking fright.

God, looking down from his Heaven said "Silly,
I've never heard such rubbish since Millie.
Put away your speakers and your old tin can,
And don't be noise pollutin', act like a man."

(But old Satan, called The Devil came up from behind
And whipped up the volume before anyone paid him mind.)
That's how it stands today, Rock is a sin,
But I might just get a little before Armageddon begins.

Retirement

She got up early in the morning
He sat in the bedroom
She swept and cleaned, washed clothes
He sat in the kitchen
She dug the earth and watered plants
He sat in the garden
She prepared the dinner and fed the pets
He sat in the dining room
Suddenly, she died
He sat in the living room.

Height of Summer

Under a plastic garden chair
A pebble, like a pendulum
Swings on a single spider's thread,
Turning, sometimes in elliptical loops,
Sometimes hanging still again.
The spider, who fooled himself,
Thinking he'd attached to solid earth,
Tries to anchor and tense.
But to no avail. He's
Hidden from view beneath the seat,
And the cat, asleep, shows no concern.

I'm not in love

I'm riding the bus,
thinking of lovers and friends,
all those chances missed,
all those nights and days,
the times I could have married,
the mad, destructive times.
Bus rides make me randy
and I could have seen you!
But who cares?
I'm not in love.

I'm walking the street;
not many people out tonight,
shop windows with clothes
showing fantasy, well-dressed people;
people, you were never like that!
There's a girl and a boy,
arms linked, talking quietly,
it could have been me, or you.
But why worry ?
I'm not in love.

I'm coming home to you,
looking forward to you,
my old wound and confusion,
(what is the matter with me?)
seem balmy tonight,
with air singing quietly,
and I'm not afraid,
I could have been you!
But what the hell
I'm not in love.

Golden Orioles

On cloudy days
The sea air is Bracing
Where the Golden Oriole flies;
Above the meadow,
Over the track
That leads to the Caravans.

Like patchwork,
The paving slabs,
Recycle bins, plant pots,
Compost makers
Lie in the lee of the woods.

On cloudy days,
When the breeze blows strong,
The little windmill buzzes and whirrs,
Beside the pond,
Above the Caravans
Where the Golden Orioles fly.

"Hejira" in Horncastle

Joni's "Amelia" happened for me.
It wasn't jet plane streams, though,
Just the early evening sunlight
Peeking through my Venetian blind
Making six lines of sunset
On my wall, above the bookshelves.
"The hexagram of the Heavens",
"The strings of my guitar";
This wasn't a "false alarm",
But a reminder of where we are.

The wall is dark now
Where that illumination chanced
To draw my eyes. I can't
Look at the sky any more;
Neither is the door always open.
Your poor companion is tired
of lies and "bloody-mindedness".
To be plain, a beer in Bath
is not a preference, only
Hell, or Heaven, whichever I find here.

HAIKU

Climbing the mountain
I saw it there: a bucket
With a hole in it!

My breathing sounds like
cold wind in northern mountains.
Suddenly I wake.

Cool summer sunset;
Watching wind and branches beat
Out polyrhythms.

I'm frightened by time;
diary and wristwatch help
to keep it at bay.

Time is like a tree;
Its branches spread through the years.
Quickly it's over!

Changes - creeping to
God; I light my fire in hope
Of your forgiveness.

He opened his eyes,
Looked at me and said, "Hi!", the
Night before he died.

As the kettle sings,
Applause on the radio;
Crackling together

The clock does not go:
No time passes as we sit
Around playing games.

reading haiku I
light a cigarette~ music
on the radio

Thoughts run like a
river. I sit in a tree
and watch them flowing.

The rain is falling
and I am eating an apple.
Peace and quiet now.

Hitching alone

the long and lonely road
i was so cold, so cold
waiting for a lift;
anybody, anyway
to pick me up,
take me anywhere.

i was mad i tell you,
i tried too hard
to get away

but about midnight, every time,
some promise of warmth and a future
would turn me round,
i'd cross the road
and beg the stars to forgive me,
grant me a safe passage
home.

Itlopa

there are backwaters of this town
where poets live and learn;
artists complete their drawings,
and my heart begins to yearn

for the good days, the wild days
we spent by the sandy sea:
we were so in love, sweetheart,

i live in your lee,
you protect me,
don't forget me,
please don't set me free.

Lecture in a dream

"What of the future?",
he asked us.
"We do not know what it is".
A black hole opened up for me,
sitting in my note-taking chair,
but then,("It is certainly not here and now"),
he brought me down to earth.
Other students shuffled restlessly.
"And fate?
Fate is interwoven fibres,
like your hands clasped together".
I looked at mine,
little fingers bent inwards,
(alas, like old Grandpa Sam,
who brought them down to me
I will never play the violin well);
showed them to my neighbour.
It was suddenly clear:
I must face fate
with three fingers
on each hand.

Life story/Lunaire

I tell you
I was born insane.
I laughed just before I died.
I was crying,
throwing diamonds
from the water,
interrupted by nuts
and iron-clad reality,
in which I never had a share
all my short, sweet life.
Pitch poured from the sky,
frightened me,
but it was only the beginning,
and as the gods made war
I ran.
Now my feet are free,
and in the end
there is nothing
but "a finger pointing
to the moon".

Love in Green

And the trees made love:
Roots and branches
Entwining together,
Beneath the Earth,
Above the Sky.

Flowers mosaiced
A carpet;
For trees that fell;
A place to lie.
The green grass grew

All around,
Mosses softened
The ground.
In the woods
The only sound
Was of gentle rain falling,
And the swish, swish
Of rushes in the wind.

Love poem no.14

The heart of our house beats audibly.
You are preparing curry.
I am drinking beer.
Everything is very still.
The cat crosses the kitchen floor,
Beethoven sounds and you chop onions.
You're slimmer now, I secretly like that.
Your hair is tied back in a bow.
You are wearing those trousers.
I want to photograph you,
Paint you,
Write a love song for you
I do believe in you, and I love you
So.

Report

A crowd gathered round
The literary casualty.
"Let me through,
I am a poet!", I pleaded.

I examined the prose form carefully.
After I had splinted his severed sentence
And had assured the onlookers
That such alliterations are perfectly normal

I consigned him to
The local Library
For contemplation and convalescence.

"All in a day's righting",
                        I thought.

Peace

The flower of happiness,
fed by medication and music
blossoms, though briefly,
and I feel good; no trembles, no pain;
light and yellow-golden,
in my room, at this end of a day.

Overlord, your fence is too high

It is a green-grabbed, pierced plain
In the British acid rain
Where the bald, pink chickens sing
About all any/everything.
The black feathered dancer King
Steps onto a red mud mound:
Arrows in war are flying,
and children are lost and found.

Down from the gas-fired kitchen
The uniforms are grey,
The cats stalk in the moonlight,
And we are going away.
The open-headed monolith
Surveys all ecstasy,
But things are going very wrong,
And I don't have a key.

Landlord, hear my broken bass;
When will you learn to see?
This is not your only place,
Can't you let us be free?
I'm wasted on my shakin' feet
I have no voice to sing,
But I will light a cigarette,
And be gone in the morning.

Up village, where the play begins
The motor cars stand round,
A silver coin lies, glistening
Upon wet, amber ground.
Judith lies asleep alone
In some far-off town:
Nothing stirs, the lights are lit,
I hear no other sound.

The hospital stands, grey and white
On grounds of countryside,
And you and I will meet someday
In fishtown on the tide.
Now I go up and you go down;
It has always been this way;
I need once more to hear the hound
Of Golden 'Frisco Bay.

On a Midsummer Eve

In this little, brick country town,
Swallows wheeling high above in
The blue-and-white, vaulted arch of the sky,
Which, like an eiderdown surrounds
The sun, a golden head
Lying sleeping
On a cloudless pillow.

Midsummer Marriage

When Daisy Green
Married Breeze Westerley
Their Priest, the Sun
Shone brilliantly,
And butterflies, like confetti
Fluttered all around.
Her dress was formed of feathers
Cast by birds in flight;
She wore tree blossom in her hair.

Cow parsley stood to attention,
And the trees formed a Guard of Honour
By the path that leads
To the Forest Grove.
Light dappled through
Onto the grassy ground.

Men had built a stone wall,
Which was their Altar:
They prayed by the pond,
Then they ate wild berries and broke bread
For their Wedding Feast.

They live in the Sky.
They live on the Earth.
They live.

Man on the road

His soul rides with me
Looking for music
For the music of the bush
That he came from
For the music of the city
That he came to
And bought a black and silver machine
For the music of the stars
That wheeled above his head
On the road that night
The night he died;
Red blood on black skin.

We were travelling late
A swinging lantern alerted us.
Stopping, we were pleaded with,
"Take him to hospital".

Children, we were frightened
We watched as his body was
Lifted into the back
On top of trunks, toys, tins of food
We covered him with a blanket.

Miles later the groaning stopped

My soul rides the music
The music of the wheels I fear
The music of the bush and the blues
The music of Classical Europe
The music
    of the
        stars.

A Bee on a Lupin

A bee on a lupin,
flying flower to flower,
forcing its way between all petals,
fucking each bloom
with its abdomen, drinking
every drop of nectar;
finally falling to the earth
beneath, too heavy to go home.

Alone
(I was sane for 15 minutes)

My tongue and my pen
Have brought me more trouble
Than breaking the law
Ever did.

Self seeking,
Pleasure loving,
Music oriented:
A man of my time.

We should shout the truth
From roof to road;
I have stood aloof,
And this has showed

That what I find in solitude
Will always be less
Than any togetherness,
And now I ache
       for your caress.

A Quick One

I'm at the bar
Of the Morning Star,
I order a pint
And wait for my glasses
To demystify
Observing the wares
On display

Nuts, I consider cashews
Or pistachios.
Bananas, in terms of the
Order of the brain
Are notable by their absence.

A cognitive Crisp
Would be welcome,
Or a mental Murphy's;
But I'm soon out of here

(The natives are becoming restful).

Autumn

another car swishes by this wet night
and my concern is war and all that's wrong;
i don't want to die yet, nor fight
but sometimes i have trouble singing along.

softly in the breeze the willow leaves fall;
do but a few know peace or can we all?

spirits flit from mountainside and moor
to valley foliage still green and kind;
i know there is God, and that's for sure
but sometimes i have trouble making up my mind.

Benedict

I sat next to him;
a return journey for me.
I told myself,
"Don't talk, life's too
tragic for that".
He stared at me,
but as I glanced into his blue eyes
he turned his head swiftly away.

I tried telepathy,
thinking, "it's o.k., Benedict,
its me, Tim from years ago" -
but there lies our mutual illusion
and there was no reply.

He limped
away from the bus stop;
I remembered that
he was the one
who would go the rounds
of ward after ward,
taking orders for
sweets, cigarettes, canned drinks:
he would walk to the shop
despite the pain.

Was he heading for a
hostel for homeless
or a squalid bedsit somewhere?
His shabby coat and
torn sweatshirt showed that
life has not been so kind
to each of us
emigres from the asylum.

Cities

I am suffused and twisted:
Old Maudlin made me this way,
my life stands, like a lecture on hate
and I do not dream my time away.
Musicians and their mates
bore me only when they talk;
I am in love with Sanctity
and I dare not walk
towards the Light for fear
of utter, inextinguishable bliss.
They did not tell me, then,
that life would be like this!
(echoes; morning thuds of glass
upon the sun-baked tarmac
are only reminders of the trance
this city wears like a mask.)
La Primavera, lure me not too slow
or I will die of hate
and, when we laughing go
to where the dance starts late,
remind me once again of cities
and their black-ribbon, endless rush,
and slow me down, make me wise
to tales of a "burning bush".

Blackpool

The lift flips
Up and down the tower
As we eat our chips
Waiting for the hour
When we'll see the sights
Of the lights at night.

Cow Bank

Butterflies and brambles;
Moths and tropical grasses;
Someday maybe
Bamboo and bulrushes
Will grow here.
The trees are lush,
Drunk on light.
Turning a corner -
An empty space, suddenly,
In the sun.

Don't Do Drugs

Friend of mine came to call
He lived in a picture on the wall
Came down each day to light his fire
And wished he'd never felt his old desire
To space out, go floating across the sky
Inside, be beautiful and never want to die.

He's too old now, you would say mature
To mess up his mind with drugs any more
Every day he comes round to speak to me
To spill out words of long-felt misery.

I'm just the same as this friend of mine
Years ago I had a yen to draw a line
Leading down to that, I was into a high time
But today, two arms and legs and half a brain
I wish I had my chance again
Then maybe now, middle aged, I'd still be sane.

Eternity

The war to end all wars,
The crashing final chord,
The breaking of the tape
At the end of the race,
The last page of the fiction,
The stone that stands at the close
Of life, blessed few words
At the service end.
I can't help believing
Despite all these:
Nothing is over, life is eternal
As the seas, the trees, the breeze.

Falling in love on buses and trains

People glimpsed across the aisle,
A woman in a wheelchair, facing me
All the way to the city - she had somehow become
More than a woman - she was a lady:
How I fell for her, and how I'll never see her again.

Love, that sweet illusion, that feeling;
An adhesive that holds me to you,
My guardian angel, strong enough (so far)
To link us through all the thick and thin we've known.

The pounding of my heart as I lie alone,
The sinister, yet beautiful night my only companion
Until sleep casts it's velvet coverlet over my mind.

Music: the love I chose as a child;
Supportive in dissipation and a refuge
When all is dark. And I can give love
With six strings and my heart.

The Universal Guru who
Teaches me more each day,
Creating compassion in my breast for all beings.

Perhaps all this is what I choose
To call "love". It's careless
As, climbing a mountain,
I turn a corner and fall
Back, slap, head-over-heels again.

26/4/94

Somehow my love for you
Has grown big, immense,
Unbounded, I want to
Shout my soul's joy
From mountain peak
To forest roof; we sit here
Quietly like the middle-aged
Lost souls we are. I had
Never been married before,
and soon it will have been
A year, or five, depending on
How you look at it. Oh words,
Damn words, they never express
A thing, I simply want to
Sing, wordlessly, a lament
For all lost souls, for all
Starving children, bleeding soldiers,
For all free people; today
Is the first day of multi-racial
Elections in S. Africa, I want
To write my love a letter, I
Daren't believe it's beginning to work,
But maybe, maybe, love can
Save the world.

1967 Revisited

You were the innocent virgin,
And he the drugged-up layabout
Your parents dreaded your meeting,
Because he'd "drag you down to his
Level", once he'd won your confidence.
So - you resisted his feeble attempts at
Instigating friendship; love was quite
Out of the question, and when he left
After a week of trying, everyone breathed a
Huge sigh of relief. What a wonderful
Effect he had. You now don't give out your
Phone number, you don't go to 'dangerous'
Places, and you would never again entertain
A man with long hair.
You are Secure.

(he's on Social Security).

whenever
the poet rises
he thinks
of drinks
and words
to drink by
what does he think by?
does he fly?
"gimme rye whiskey
or i'm gonna die"

yesterday
brought a bottle
snapped a mouthful
said it was lies

i got no time for you
got to
get those blues
out of my
glass till i'm dry

Where there's Help there's Hope

Help! Help! there's someone alive in here.
You come and go, joking,
happy and complete.
You're older now and tired,
you wonderful, loving people.
I didn't reject you, it was
illness made me pale and bland.

Help! Help! there's someone alive in here.
You feel you can't give anymore,
to one so wrongheaded.
You put on your smile,
you talk down.
I smile back, yes, it's me,
I used to understand.

Help! Help! there's someone alive in here.
Years ago, we used to laugh
together and you'd tell me
your heart and soul:
I remember, it's still precious to me,
I want to hold out a hand.

Help! Help!
I need you to trust me.

Help! Help!
Don't stop loving me.

Help! Help!
I'm still alive in here!

walking man

a zen walking meditation;
he calmed the whole ward,
serenity flowing from his long hair
as he paced up and down
          up and down
the smoking room ⁄⁄

More from the Smoke Room

No Zen walks these;
but two men frantically treading
round and around each other,
while Madonna and Stravinsky
make love
out of time
on two simultaneous radios.

Wait for no man

Quiet time
disquietens me;
no pauses, no gaps,
but hesitation for
lessthanasecond
causes my heart to stand,
as the secondhand
leaps across a watchface,
notching up regularity again.

Tides flow as I go
back again to see;
chilling breezes shock me awake,
my eyes cry and my feet freeze,
all is well as life passes on,
evading the final issue as long
as possible, no pauses, no gaps.

Happiness, my goal eludes;
pain punctuates,
giving way to ecstasy
when all is still.
Giving love - thinking positively;
more than this is not human,
but we can be free.
And we can **fly!**

Voice

You're not me
you don't sound like me
You don't speak like me
You don't think like me

I hear you
You speak to me
You think for me
You think against me

You are in my head
You are singing in my ear
You are clear
You are more me

Than I am myself.

TIME

In the last diary statement
apprehension that it was the end of time
inside my darkness is still in doubt
fear of the end of life
and yet nothing to fear
this human ambiguity

I'm sure that outside of me
everything's peaceful and
infinitely comfortable
in timeless continuity

Five senses,
my perceived three dimensions
and my assumed fourth -
my brain screams
with the pain of
everything inside.

Creativity:-
a libido induced hormonal activity.
Love:- a libido induced hormonal activity.
Togetherness:- a libido induced hormonal perception.
Peace:-
a libido induced hormonal perception.
TIME:- a libido
    induced?
        hormonal?
            assumption?
a victim of myself
...funny my name...

Two Homes

My grandparents owned a house like this one;
Now a psychiatric hostel
Where I find myself "chilling out".
My mind goes back to my uncle's wedding, a grand affair,
And I imagine cocktail parties held here
In 1920s elegance, spilling into the garden
Where once was a lake, where rhododendrons still bloom.

The oak panelled walls, stuccoed cornices, ceiling roses
Are still here.
What interactions, lovemaking, disputes
Are now past?

What irony, that one "driven mad"
By those who envied his father's wealth
And who hated his wisdom
Should now be enjoying this house as respite
From his shrunken life!

T.V.'s on most of the time of course,
But when all's quiet I play R.3 or Classic F.M.,
They don't seem to mind
And my dreams retreat to Meadows:
My uncle practicing on the grand,
The dark aroma of cigar smoke
And the donkeys out back, crossbacked,
Still carrying Christ.

Meadows - the name of my grandparents' house in Surrey
which I visited sometimes.

The unknown musician

burnt in his cabbage patch tie
notes on the future lie
wrapped around, all around
he didn't want to die

nothing can shift him, they said
as they paced the ground around
if he'd died of a riff, note dead
he wouldn't have made a sound

but he'd died of his music sleeping
it had pierced him to the floor
all those forgotten years weeping
who would want more?

The World Inside Your Eye

You don't often look at me
for long, so when you did,
just now, I looked back intent,
without a smile.

I saw a whole world;
a seahorse beckoned me
to enter, travel the sea
to where the Phoenix rises
and Pegasus brings his wings.

Then you smiled and blinked
and I quickly died,
seeing no more
the world inside your eye.

The Snake

The snake that lives
in our sitting room
coils around us, numbing
our toes and fingers,
making my flesh creep
with each criticism
of what we do.

I put on another CD
and crawl wordlessly
across the room to
the warmer heart of you.

The Moose

There is a moose in my
    record player.
His antlers stick through
    the speakers.
He dances on the mantelpiece,
    hooves going,
clickety-clack, trit-trot.
He wore my white trousers
    for breakfast
this morning, said he enjoyed
    the toast,
danced in my clogs
then returned to the turntable.
I wonder if he has a wife
but he looks the born bachelor.
Someday I'm going to get him out
    of here
before he eats my best
    pressed flowers
(a few are gone, but most remain)
and send him to Antarctica
for a long holiday with
    the Russians.
Perhaps he could join the K.G.B.
or be a double agent
    if he's lucky.
I think he's spying on behalf
of the local Supermarket M.D.
but he doesn't know everything.
I mustn't let him catch on
    I suspect;
(keep this poem secret.)

The Oak and the Elm

You and I are eight years old today
And I'm wondering will this first of May
Bring any change to Governmental power?
This is not our first, but our eleventh hour.

The sun shone warm this day,
We <u>did</u> go out to play;
Took a cruise from Scarborough Bay,
Yes, this is our first of May!

Her Majesty, for whom I drink and smoke
Like us, sees this not as a joke,
Nor a dress rehearsal for folk;
(outside our window, the Elm and the Oak).

You and I now are married four years,
We have shared joys, and fears, and tears,
And love, if they'd really like to know.
Don't let me <u>ever</u> let you go.

The evening of two angels

Wandering, I was lost
In a dark tunnel or more than one
With no light to be seen,
Even the moon was black.
I waited for her for an eternity,
Then she opened the door.
I trembled for hours talking to her,
Then finally she spoke.
Her words were like the cream
That sits on your kitchen table,
And I, the cat was allowed to drink at last.
This angel I left, saying "Thank you" and "Goodbye".
I will go back again, not for more cream,
But to show her how well fed and plump I am, I will become.
I returned to my cradle,
And another angel's voice appeared.
He told me to gain more cream,
He told me what was special about cream,
He told me how to drink until I am fat,
Until I am nearly sick.
And now I thirst, but I know forever,
And I have recourse to angels,
And I will drink more cream.

Sunday at 6

You think I've changed, don't you?
Looking out on the tiny spider,
Making its way across the tablecloth;
I, who was your minstrel Romeo
now sadder, wiser, closer to home,
I, who garlanded your bed with flowers,
and who drank wine with you by moonlight,
who now craves his 6 o'clock sherry
and expects the Sunday meal to grace his table.

Where are we bound for, you and I?
One more step along a highway
On which there is no-one but you,
And I will not fail for weeping;
Though I may fall, I will pick myself up,
And mark time in my diary.
Your hair falling catches my eyes
and your eyes are the stillest blue
and I love you more than words can tell;
I will forever worship you.

Song of the Seasons

Summer:
we met, touched,
kissed, fell in love
against a whitewashed wall.
the sun was hot,
we drank lager in cafes,
drenched in each other.

in Autumn
I rode trains to see her,
slept in a strange bed
eiderdowned with flowers,
watched TV
and drank sherry
before the Sunday roast.

Winter:
I lost her,
speaking of another lover
she sprang from my side
and pain filled the gap between us
with blood and bones.

in Spring
I telephoned
with piano blues,
remembering summer
not "out there" in France
with the whitewash heat
but in a corner of my mind,
reflected.

The Devil Came Up Here

The Devil came up here
So close he could almost touch
Me in my little house,
Frightened of demons and such.

The Devil took me walking
Through woods and over fields.
He told me I was special,
A One who dealt in deals.

The Devil's gone away now,
And I'm writing sober lines;
Pale blues and greens are all that's
Left me, gone are bright colours
        of former times.

Love in the afternoon

Bach sings
the bird rises
the lark brings
Good tidings
Overflowing refrains
tell me
time's to love again
well the
love's there
if you care
to follow it
to the hollow
warm and dark
in nature's park
where we can find
peace of mind.
Bach rings
the lark sings
the park brings
home outdoors
closer over
Lonely moors
down woven
paths into
dark sunshine. ⁄⁄

Winter

One honeysuckle leaf
suspended from the branch
by a single spider's thread spins
in the sharp air.
It is winter, and nobody goes
into the summerhouse,
the twig over the door is not disturbed;
the string from which the leaf hangs
is not broken:
perhaps it will not be severed
until spring comes.

Schizophrenia

Thoughts flash across the horizon.
My father tells me, telepathically
that, "You Do, Don't You", and I know
I do, and I agree. I feel
ill and want to vomit but
I can only cough. "Too many
cigarettes", my mother tells me
(again in my head) and yet coughing
is the only way to clear my mind.

I look out of the window,
the grass is black and the sky is pink,
but only for a moment, too short
to call them beautiful; then everything
is boring and I'm seeing though
the wrong end of a telescope.
My lucky number is 9, and I was
nine when I first heard a voice;
it said "No, Don't!", and I weep.

The people on the mag's cover
are talking to me. I. try not to
respond, hoping for a breakthrough
into the light that doesn't break down.
Inside the pages remind me there is
starvation, war, disease. I write
and hope people see fragmented
pieces of me, my disease is
under control, and inside her, lies love.

Rising dreams like

woven screams the
starlight gleams through
where I lie.
Feeling good the
colour of wood the
knowing I should like
not to die.
Girls reveal their
bodies feel my
vibes are real and
catch my eye.
Sandals on into
the sun and
all is one under
the sky.
In my sleep I
see so deep I
never weep some-
times I fly.

Machine

I have seen the machine, the dark machine.
The dogs growled in their sleep
While I stood and derided the "truth",
Seeing the machine, the demon dog machine.

When I was a little boy, the machine
Threatened (in my feverish nightmare)
To turn the world upside down; my hands
Were huge and inflated; I ran for the shelter
Of my mother's arms. Now my whole body
Feels that unreality at times, my mind
Split from its anchor in the here-and-now.

I tell people, and thus have few friends,
Few as loyal as you. I have seen timelessness,
The 4th dimension. I know the promises are
                 coming
                      true.

In an Asian Restaurant

flowing saris
dusty streets
elephants and
spicy meats

dhotis on dirzees
shalwar kemise
turbans and kirpans
jellabi sweets

my mind's eye
feasts on these
here at my table
enjoying Indian ease

Afternoon Daymare

Their mouths are
Dry as dust,
their clawed feet rattle
on stone floors;
scattering hither and thither
they seek out ants and flies;
black, watering holes
fill with their lies.

Cats cry in the moonlight
and screen ghosts
force their way closer,
more intrusive, telepathically
poised to steal thoughts,
read every insight,
insert messages I don't understand.
This is Sunday in sunshine.

They are closing in. ◢

After Caravaggio
(for MW)

Paint, my friend.
your blood in colours
of rainbow
on your canvas skin.
I have learnt to be cruel,
she weeps
and I do not know
how to stop.
We are dead
    yes
    but breathing,
our eyes blind
    behind spectacles
our feet do not touch this Earth.
My hand
would stroke her hair
my fingers touch her eyelids
the pain is there
it is forever
This is my sanity.

Aunt Susan, your bones twisted
hawthorn twigs
coughing in tears,
did you know that I slept with Tony's wife
smoked pot beneath Milton's tree,
masturbated in the morning
before school?
Pottery figures
on your corner shelves,
static, shining,
your life with the T.V.
Did you guess she would cry like this?
I do not know
how to stop.

Nec Spe
Nec Metu
I feel this
as, like the clock on the wall
I watch my life tick away.
I have suffered
Les Quatre Cent Coups
bitten by a lizard
I was aged five,
Kicked mercilessly into submission
I was twenty four,
cups of tea
this is my sanity.
I love you, you beautiful artist
and I will hold your paintings
in my eyes.

Music stroke Light

   In music
which is silence
made radiant by sound
   I see light
making radiant
   darkness.
I could not understand
   music
until I saw
   chaos
I could not understand
   light
until I heard
   screams.
And what I feel
is music forever
making love to light
when I touch your cheek
to wipe away a tear.

Alchemy

My thoughts
are on the videotape,
as Knopfler picks
my visions,
tracking back
with contemplations
of his own.

Meanwhile he sings
of Shakespeare's lovers.

I'm "wired for sound";
electrodes
link my brain
to his National guitar;
street serenading
an imaginary jewel –

as might be found
on a Sultan's turban.

London, centre
of the musical world,
and its streets,
now home to Rock n Roll,
of you I dream
at crossroads

where many have met
and from which

some have flown.

In appreciation of your "lofty pathos"

Professor, drink up your beer,
play the piano for us,
we want to dance.
And when I die, bearded man
I want your atheistic prayer
to go with me, follow me,
down that cobbled, German street
I have seen only on postcards,
where I will leap.

Viel Bier trinken und
Zigaretten rauchen, lying back
in that meadow
100 years ago,
regretting your childlessness
(I regret mine also).

I know only those warm chords,
Johannes, and your kindness,
greatness of spirit and your
soaring insight will always haunt me.
I would free myself from very love
if I could find, through that
such expanses,
such flight
in my scribblings.
Today, in sunshine,
in the rippling air of summer
I have found at least
a small comer to stand in.

*The composer Johannes Brahms, as a young man, would supplement his income by accompanying (on the piano)dancers in bars and cafes.

40 line poem/music in 40 parts
"I have nothing to say, and I am saying it" - John Cage

You do not know
what darkness lies
beyond that black square
(gold threads link me
to my heart, my mind,
to the artist;
who draws me, wooing me
with his soft pen
closer and closer).
I do not fear it now,
that awesome descent
that remains a threat,
but fills my eyes.

Sentences are not like equations;
they have a linear meaning
and grow as they travel.
Your blank mind.
Your television, soft porn nights.
You do not ask me
what I see.

You know the warmth
of sun,
but you do not see the light
(arcing in 7am midsummer
blue cloudless sky through
windows that hurt my eyes;
a screaming
rock 'n' roll guitar
woke you from your bed
and there were complaints).
You hear the sound
but you did not fear the night
and when snow came
I did not feel you rejoice.

Friend, I drink with you,
I eat with you, I breathe with you;
when I hear with you, see with you,
and you, and you, and you... ◢

Three Ages

I am a small child
I am cradled on your knee
I feel the back of my head
Against your beard
I know the warmth of your love
We are watching a chimpanzee
Outside and listening to the
Ticking of your watch.

I am a grown man
I am far away from you
I have contracted a mental illness
All I ever loved has gone
I have taken an overdose
I am waiting for sleep
It is night and I am alone
There is nothing left.

I am middle-aged now
I am sitting with her
I can see her cradled
Against the back of the chair
I can feel the warmth of her love
We are writing poetry
Of intoxication and listening to the
Music I have always loved

since I was a child with you.

Meeting with Pan

He was golden,
with green ears,
his mellow yellow legs
were hung with leaves.
His hair fell like soft grass
upon his barky brow,
and his naked body
was covered with foliage;
red flowers
on his breast.
He walked with a slow,
creaking gait,
all eight feet or so of him
gliding gently
across the city pavement,
over the road
towards me.
He looked so peaceful;
I said "hello",
and walked with him
down long, empty, black-and-red
streets of Leeds,
as he sang sadly, softly,
of new juggernauts,
harsh concrete,
and a Golden.Age long ago.
We walked toward the river,
and he sat on the bank,
dipping his green, mossy feet
into the water.
There was a loud splash
as I turned away,
and ripples smacked the shore.
One saggitate leaf
bobbed, and flowed gently downstream.

thinking man

a man wanders round
my body, once transparent,
now flesh and blood again,
connecting words and images
i see in dreams and when
i close my eyes in strange
and unbelievable ways
to make the stories i tell
more interesting, witty.

before, when he was not there,
I thought in straight lines.
he tricked me into letting him in
by saying there was a gun in my mouth
- then jumping down the barrel.
now i think laterally, along
side roads, down deserted corridors
and out to the deep,
        blue
           sea.

Community Care

The very place I always dreaded
when fear consumed my mind,
(in my hidden nightmare
I would be dragged there,
passive, inwardly screaming)
became a sanctuary,
a place of beauty, tranquility, peace,
until it began to shrink,
slowly at first, as we were
expelled to the world,
to win or fail as we might
(some died in fright); tentacles
from that place once supported us
but have now vanished from our sight.

We have nowhere to go,
our homes (if we're lucky),
graveyards for our minds,
or 'public places', pitched battlefields
where we beg for help
from the sidelines. Pubs feed us
addictive anaesthetics , take our money ;
sometimes we're hungry, sometimes we kill.

Who can we turn to?
Doctors offer us extra downers,
(complicating our cocktails)
to tranquilise and soothe;
warm human contact is more expensive.
We're all alone in here,
invaded by unreal tormentors we cannot see
and cannot control.

When I saw your face again

Surprised to find you on the stairs
I climbed up to your room behind you
I wanted to say I still love you
You know I wanted to say that
But I didn't dare
We went out, I in my hat
You in your hood
You opened a bank account while I waited
You know I was only doing what I felt I should
Looking after you, the day you came out of hospital
Where was the picture you painted?
Of yourself, the one I wept seeing last night
Can I explain the way I felt through the rain?
It was torrential
I remember visiting you in fright
And you kissed me that day on the lips
I was surprised to see you on the landing
And when I saw your face again,
it could have launched a thousand million starships
I bent over and still standing
I kissed your surprised mouth.

Sunday Afternoons

As I look out on this
Wet Saturday afternoon;
Church tomorrow,
A taxi back to the ward
After that, I think of Leeds.
Thirty years of living in
Black-and-red streets,
No money, wet Sunday
Afternoons.

That dark flame that
'Is forever England' still
Burns in my heart;
I ran down the path towards
The future, found only
Nothingness, but a lost
Youth, a girl
Called me back,
Back, back to my country,
The Kabaka's Kingdom,
My home.

Desecration, the bullet,
The bomb, the trucks
Carrying gangs of youths
Heavily armed,
Never willing to surrender,
Even to their death; always
Ready to steal, kill.

There is a secret I
Dare not tell. All is not
As evil as it first
Seems, dreams that turn into
Nightmares can turn back,

Back, back to sunshine
Wine, roses;
To pleasant countryside
On Sunday afternoons.

Footnote:
The Kabaka - King of Uganda.

Scene

Parading through the garden;
Stately figures dressed in robes.
Finery is all around,
Grace abounds,
Dignity of gentility floats in the air.

Your knowledge, your works,
The profound and the absurd,
Sensuality of words;
Power hovers
Like a hawk, ready to descend.

I sit and gaze, amazed,
Writing another fleurette.
Read my lines,
Hear my rhymes,
I know my own place now, here.

Will you take my hand, lover?
Breathe the scented, dewy air.
Find intoxication
Mellows you

As musicians play our earthsong.
All who are here are sleeping;
Dreaming life as it could be.
Sweet illusions
Friends of mine,
Sublime reflections in your days.

Skyscene

Flowers are like clouds
Floating over wild, blue hills.
Swallows' shadows swoop
On hard, arid ground:
The sound
Of the sun beating down
Is silence for your mind. ⁄⁄

Other publications available from Stairwell Books

First Tuesday in Wilton	Ed. Rose Drew and Alan Gillott
The Exhibitionists	Ed. Rose Drew and Alan Gillott
The Green Man Awakes	Ed. Rose Drew
Fosdyke and Me and Other Poems	John Gilham
frisson	Ed. Alan Gillott
Gringo on the Chickenbus	Tim Ellis
Running With Butterflies	John Walford
Late Flowering	Michael Hildred
Scenes from the Seedy Underbelly of Suburbia	Jackie Simmons
Pressed by Unseen Feet	Ed. Rose Drew and Alan Gillott
York in Poetry Artwork and Photographs	Ed. John Coopey and Sally Guthrie
Rosie and John's Magical Adventure	The Children of Ryedale District Primary Schools
Her House	Donna Marie Merritt
Taking the Long Way Home	Steve Nash
Chocolate Factory	Ed. Juliana Mensah and Rose Drew
Skydive	Andrew Brown
Still Life With Wine and Cheese	Ed. Rose Drew and Alan Gillott
Somewhere Else	Don Walls
49	Paul Lingaard

For further information please contact rose@stairwellbooks.com

www.stairwellbooks.co.uk